Fru Hypomania

Brown Santa

© 2019 by Sarabjeet Singh Gill

———

Published by Guddi Publishing

———-

All Rights Reserved

Manufactured in the United States of America

Cover design: Sarabjeet Singh Gill

ISBN: 9781074581404

Fruits of
Hypomania

Poems by

Brown Santa

(Sarab Gill)

Fruits of Hypomania / Brown Santa

Acknowledgment

I can write a whole new book to appreciate people whom I want to acknowledge in making this book a reality. I don't know where to start and end. I use to write those cheesy breakup poems during my teenage years and was out of touch with any sort of serious effort towards writing until 2015.

Goya Robles, my teacher galvanized me to write poetry and introduced me to Da Poetry Lounge. I can never thank him enough for the love, trust, and talent he showered upon me.

I am forever grateful to Da Poetry Lounge for letting me be in the space of nurture for the Broken ones. They made this Immigrant boy feel at home. The safe space they have for everyone beyond borders, colors, and race is what, a lost soul like me could have wished for. The Next Tuesday is what I live for, for the past 3 years. If it wouldn't have been for DPL, I never would have found my voice and channelize it the way I am able to do it now. So, thank you DPL for everything.

Thank you, Mom and Dad, for letting me be who I am. I couldn't have asked for anything different. Thank you for putting up with this lunatic troublemaker who made your life hell most of the time.

Thank you Diljot, my little brother for loving me unconditionally and I love you like no one can love anyone.

Thank you "Gurpreet Veere" for being the big brother I needed in life. You never failed to be there in thick n thin.

And I extend my deepest gratitude to the almighty for all the above and beyond.

Fruits of Hypomania / Brown Santa

Contents

1)

Poems

Isn't that fucked-up?

My passion

Genetically

He

Time traveler

Pray

Patience

Failure

That kind of love

Vision

Favor

Fear and Freedom

Hammers and nails

A Day-off

Boys don't cry

The Poet

2)

Art

Goddess of muse

The seed of muse

One day

Imperfections

Or

Crawl

Storms

My fingers bleed

A spell untold

Handful of sand

Lap three

3)

Take me by the anchor

Let me call you an itch

We both love ice-cream

Your boomerang

We both are in love

I am not afraid

Dummy

AND BUT

You just don't know

Bullshit

Expert

Courage

God is great

And over

Pay attention

Messed it up

Because of you

I need to learn

4)

COUGH

Character

FOTB

Some people hate life

Born undocumented

Journey towards you

I wasn't myself

Tomorrow

Let go

Religion

Religious

Mirage of life

Intentions

Tragedy

Your charities

5)

Dodging a bullet.

Gandhi

Poems, I can never write.

Fruits of Hypomania / Brown Santa

Fruits of Hypomania / Brown Santa

Fruits of Hypomania / Brown Santa

Poems, They are not mine to keep.

Nor do I own them.

I don't write them. Neither I can.

They write themselves/through me.

When I force it, I end up rhyming and call it a poem.

I have a bad habit of rhyming.

I have come to a decision that if I rhyme too much,

I must know/it's a bad poem.

Those abandoned/reckless/uncouth/unconventional/ questionable/untrustworthy stories which were trying to hitchhike on my tongue/never get a ride. When I rhyme, those words get desperate to fit your ear and my voice forgets who it is serving.

It's hard to tell sometimes whether I write to express

or impress but I guess I shouldn't distress if and when I digress.

But then everything I write looks like a mess.

See!!!, I rhymed again. It's an epidemic.

It kills my zone. I hate rhyming.

There can be rhyming in poetry, but just rhyming is not poetry.

That's what I believe but then

Why the fuck should anyone give a fuck about what I believe?

Believes could be right or wrong.

Who the fuck am I to say What is what?

Isn't that, what has brought the human race

to where it is now?

Self-righteousness?

You talk different.
You walk different.
Why should I believe you?
I don't care if what you are saying makes sense or not.
I am gonna hate it because it doesn't ring a precedent in my head. And to tell you the truth, I just don't want to be wrong.
I hate being wrong.
I loathe being wrong.
So, I awarded myself THE RIGHT to be RIGHT. Always.

But, that's just me. I am sure it's just me who thinks like that.
Anyway, say hello to my poems.
They often get venerable with the wrong people at the wrong times.
They often can't decide whether to laugh at something or cry.
All I am asking is, be patient with them
They are afraid of judgment and mockery.
They are afraid of getting hurt. They are just afraid to show up.

My Poems are my baby birds and they are afraid to fly.
I don't have the heart to, but I am pushing them off the nest.
For if they won't ever take a flight/
I will never know how many more hearts/
could have been their homes.

***

Hello, my name is Brown Santa and I am fucked up.
Why am I telling you that?
cuz, therapy is expensive.

But, You know what's more fucked up, than being fucked up? Not knowing that you are fucked up.
Oh yeah, the day you admit to yourself that you are fucked up. A whole nother world opens up to you. The unknown emptiness starts making sense.
You can call it an epiphany/a revelation/enlightenment or give it some voodoo name.
It's a blessing just to know that in this perfect world, I am perfectly fucked up.
It's a blessing to know who you are and I am not afraid to admit, I am fucked up. I am wired like that.
The only difference between now and then is that;
Now, I speak outside what I use to scream inside.

Did you know, Poetry is written by fucked-up people?
Oh yeah, Poetry is written by fucked up people.
So they can share their fucked-up stories
with other fucked-up people.
I have a bad memory. Please, remind me again,
Misery seeks what?
Exactly!

Now I am not saying you are fucked up but let's keep the
option open. I will ask a few questions and you can figure
out,
If you are fucked-up or not.
Ready?

Do you rehearse comebacks for fights,
Which may or may not happen in the future?
You are what?

Do you rehearse improved comebacks from fights
which had already happened in the past?
You are what?

Do you rehearse excuses for shit that happened a month
ago?
You are what?

Do you find yourself often misunderstood
But still, feel the need to hold your tongue?
You are what?

Do you wish to go home when you are out and go out when
you are home?
You are what?

I graduated from law school in India

Packed my bags and moved to LA

Now, I have a stomach full of poems and pocket full of pennies.

I am officially fucked up!!!

But, It's ok.

This city has taught me how to walk in traffic and talk to myself, without caring who is looking.

This city has taught me the difference between lonely and solitude but nothing is free and the price has been painful.

But, it's ok.

I don't want to live in a nest made of broken dreams.

So, I am letting my dreams

break my bones

to build a nest for me.

Dreams are milestones on an unknown path and If I would have let conformity choose my path

I would have been what?

Isn't that fucked-up?

* * *

Between

STARING eyeballs

and closed minds.

My ignited heart

threads **My passion**

through the needles of life.

* * *

They always say " Just be happy"

Except, if they can explain what fuck that even means?

I can't even figure out "How to be me",

let alone be the way/you see me.

I don't believe in pursuing happiness, just to be clear

Life is not a destination, everything I need is here.

The milestones of happiness are the byproduct of the journey to freedom and freedom in the journey.

And what is happiness? if not freedom.

The freedom to be me, unapologetically.

Cuz esthetically,

This is how I am wired Genetically.

I love freedom so much, I can die for it,

I choose to just take it, rather cry for it.

I will take my freedom or you can take my life.

But I promise I won't give it up. Without a fight.

All I ever wanted was to be free. cuz I believed

When I will be free, I won't suffer, but oohhhh boy...

Stop being a boy, life ain't no toy.

Freedom doesn't promise exemption from suffering;

But time anymore doesn't feel like buffering /since I realized our existence is the fruit of our mother's labor.

We are born out of pain. But, it's the joy of creation that we live for and what is life,

if not an endless quest of Seeking blessings in disguise

So, until I come to an end

I will keep creating the children of muse, Unapologetically.

Cuz esthetically

This is how I am wired Genetically.

They always say "just be happy"

I will say it only once," Just be free"

Free from what you used to be,

Free from what everyone else wants you to be.

cuz, a seed have to stop being a seed to grow and become a tree/be what you want to be and show the world what you know, Unapologetically

Cuz esthetically

This is how we are wired **Genetically**.

***.

He whose hands,

don't hew any stone.

His life looms itself,

while he pays no heed.

***

I am here to confess

I am a **Time traveler** and I own a magic train.

My train is way ahead of its time.
Never, ever it stops.
I wake up it's running.
I go to sleep, it's still running.
Most of the times, it's running without a driver.

My train is faster than anything Elon Musk can build.
It can travel years forward or backward in nanoseconds.
But, navigation is an area I am still working on.
I mean, if you remember Apple Maps used to suck.
If they can improve, so can I.

My train is called, the "Train of Thoughts."
It's a hybrid model, running on two kinds of fuel—

Let me introduce you to Fuel#1.
It's called " The Future Dreams". This fuel is very forceful in its nature, but it lacks ignition. Running On this fuel, My train does some Transformers-kind of shit and becomes a fighter jet.
Ready to engage and destroy all enemies obstructing its way.
However, miles per gallon on this fuel are very disappointing.
But the problem lies in the composition of this fuel, itself.
This fuel is incomplete in its nature.
It's composed of 2 major elements: Imagination and Fear.

In the beginning, imagination is all over my hippocampus.
But, the molecules of fear are very strong and eats imagination
like cancer cells.

Fear - The residue from my failed endeavors
collaborates with my present circumstances
and produces so much friction with my vision
that from feeling like a star
I become a shooting star destined to hit the ground.

My fighter jet loses its flight;
Now, it's back to being a train.
(You know, the Transformers-kind of shit)

Now if I want to travel in the fighter-jet mode,
I have to add an extra element in this fuel.
— it's called "Trust."

I took a shot of trust even before publishing this book.
But, this element is just as common as common sense
so I have to dig deep for it, always.

Although fuel #1 is my go-to fuel,
but it's just as flaky as me.
if and when it runs out—
And it happens very often—
My plane switches itself to

Fuel#2

This is a highly inflammable fuel;

It has the capacity to turn my garden of roses into ashes.

It is called "Past regrets."

FYI, it's so inflammable!

It can catch fire in the blink of a memory.

The two major molecules of this fuel are "Guilt and Anger."

I have enough stock of this fuel and with each passing year,

this fuel is increasing in volume at a miraculous speed.

and when I hit 30, I realized

I have way more STOCK than I imagined.

My imagination also tells me

that there are more time-traveling mutants like me.

I am here, seeking my fellows mutants to come together

and mine more of the third missing element for

Fuel #1

cuz divided we fall

Together we fly.

* * *

In loss,

Write what you gain/

from reading your pain.

Time will erase/

Don't frown upon the stain.

Even when you have

nothing to lose or gain.

Pray,

it never goes vain.

* * *

To have meaningful answers,
I have to have meaningful questions.

To have meaningful questions,
I have to have meaningful problems.

To have meaningful problems,
I have to have a meaningful path.

To have a meaningful path,
I have to have a meaningful vision.

To have a meaningful vision.
I have to have a meaningful destination.

To have a meaningful destination,
I have to have a meaningful start.

To have a meaningful start,
I have to have a meaningful purpose.

To have a meaningful purpose,
I have to have a meaningful foundation.

To have a meaningful foundation,
I have to have Patience.

To have patience.
I have to practice **Patience**.

* * *

Failure is familiar;

Failure is a friend;

Failure is fine.

Give it to me; It's mine.

I own it like I own your pity.

I wear it under my feet,

It reminds me, it's never too late

to walk straight.

Walk straight.

Walk straight.

Walk straight,

Fearless through the gate of fate.

I apologize, I think I will fail

even to fail you.

* * *

Sometimes I forget/
if I am holding a pencil or a scapula.

Sometimes I forget/
why I write.
Let me try:
Why do I write? Why do I write? Why do I write?
I write so I can give
What I want to receive.
What do I want to receive?
Love and hate, both are contagious.

Sometimes I forget what love is!
What is love? What is love? What is love?
Let me try.
Love is rain falling on our faces
irrespective of our genetic make-up.

Love is god listening to our prayers
It doesn't care
if we join our hands or raise them in the air
as long as we get on our knees.
I don't know what love is!
Love is what we think it is,
I do know what love has done for me,
and what I can do with love to you.

To me, love is radiating light
Even when It's burning inside

Do you know
Who else burns every day
to give light?

Exactly, **That kind of love.**

* * *

If you and yourself
are not yet in collision
sooner than later
I hope, when you burn that prison
you will know,
the religion of a pigeon
is confined to its **Vision.**

* * *

Favor is a myth;

Every myth has an agenda.

If you don't see it right now,

Give it some time

and wait for this line

It's only fair if...

* * *

If you shut your eyes
The sun doesn't disappear

Fear pain and you can never be truly happy.

For, **Fear and Freedom** can't live in the same moment.

* * *

Hammers and Nails

There are days, my every endeavor,

gets hard to swallow that fails.

I look outside my window.

I see blood-ridden hammers, hunting for nails.

There are days, I can finish a book without any breaks.

Then there are days, I can write a book about my aches.

There are days, life feels like a marathon of sprints;

And I run, one after the other.

I run like I have wings,

I run like I don't remember what I was.

I will see you at the end of the tunnel,

I run like I don't plan to pause.

Then there are days, I lose my navigator.

I no longer remember,

if I am running towards something

or from something.

I get on my knees,

Tell me, where am I supposed to go, GOD?

Please...drop me some hints.

Then there are days, I feel entitled to live my life.

My goosebumps prove the shower of his blessings.

I feel like a giant ball of fire,
Ready to burn anything that comes my way.

The train headed to the land of despair is always there
to pick me up.
But, Maybe, there is a heaven on the other side of faith.
Maybe, I should stop looking
for the destination and enjoy the view.

In those days, God loves me more than I hate myself.
I end up finding parking where I never expected!
Birds start singing for me.
I feel blessed.
I am such a fool to feel rejected.
Maybe, he has a plan.
NOOOOOO!!!
He definitely has a plan; I can't yet see.
I know he is looking after me.
Perhaps, I should look back and appreciate where I was.
Maybe, just for now he is keeping me
right where I am supposed to be.

Then, there are days
I feel like a fool to believe there is something called GOD!
Does he even exist?
If he does, is he listening to me?

SIRRRRR?

MAM?

YOU THEREEEEEE?

Is God a man

a woman?

A Hermaphrodite?

Straight?

Gay?

Bi?

White?

Black?

Brown?

Yellow?

Maybe all of the above

Or none of the above

I don't know.

Sometimes my faith feels like a ship

Afraid of sinking but dying to sail.

Maybe I should fuc'in stop looking outside

All it has brought me is nothing but pain.

Perhaps, I need to look inside

once again.

* * *

I am sorry, mother.

But

if you really want

me to stop biting my nails,

I need to be taken away from me.

I need me to stop playing the scenes

in my dreams

over and over, I don't wish to see.

I wish to sleep,

at least one night,

and feel free.

I need

A day off

from

being

me.

* * *

The mother of a student of mine asked me a question about her son. "He is very sensitive and highly emotional. What do I do about this problem?

Her question made me think, how did my mother deal with this sensitive tornado since 1988? There is so much I can thank my mother for that I can write a book about it. But today I want to thank her for never tagging my sensitivity as a problem. For never telling me,

" **Boys don't cry.** You are not a girl. Be a man".

I wish I could go back in the history of mankind and find that one person whoever for the first time demanded from a boy to "STOP CRYING LIKE A GIRL, BE A MAN".

I wish I could go back and stop that chain reaction right there. Because that chain is wrapped around my gender's neck since then and we are choking on our own emotions.

"STOP CRYING LIKE A GIRL, BE A MAN"

Ok!! Fair enough.

I don't want to cry like a girl.

How about I cry like a man?

MAN TO MAN.

I don't care how mother fucking tough you think you are.

When pain surrounds you.

You hide from everyone.

Secretly Hoping for someone to say

"I found you".

But I don't want to hide.

I want you to recognize the strength I exercise when I let you witness my pain

MAN TO MAN.
What is your definition Manly MAN?
You muscular, muscular, muscular MAN.
A masculine creature who don't feel any pain because he has a dick?
Without any emotions, you ain't nothing more than a dick, MAN.
I knew everything about being a man then when I didn't know anything.
Now? I know something, That I don't know anything!
But, there's something I know about tears.
Fall in love with them, MAN
Let them touch those anguishing secluded nooks, MAN
Let them flow like rivers, MAN

When I was 15, I asked a doctor.
Why do I cry so much?
Something is wrong with me!
Can you fix me?
I am glad, he couldn't.
Tears used to wound the MAN in me.
Now, I am 31. Quite often I cry like a baby, I am more of a man than I ever was or can ever be.
But what do I know of being a MAN! I knew everything then

when I didn't know anything. Now, I know something/
that Emotions are not gender-specific like toilets.

And to the mother who asked me what do I do with my sensitive boy?
Make sure your boy grows up to be a Sensitive Man.
And tell him
"Whenever life brings you on your knees.
Don't worry about shedding leaves.
A new spring, life will bring.
Because FALL is just another Season."
Tell him that
"your emotions don't make you weak.
But, whether you drown in your tears Or you choose to swim through your fears, will decide who you are."

And you, then my MAN. MY MANLY MAN.
Whenever life happens and you want to cry?
Don't try to steer/your tears away.
Because I don't give a fuck what your gender is/ Humans are made of the same clay.
You are human before you are a man, MAN.
And it's not just your right but also your duty to act like one.

Are you listening to me Man?

* * *

There is fire.

There is not.

Solstice of life

feels tattered, yet young.

A love song, Unsung.

My fierce wings in murky bars,

have real dreams to fly far.

Whoever said "Dreams are Free,"

Lied to you and me.

There's a price you'll find,

eclipsed under my scars.

There is fire;

there is not.

Death at dusk,

Resurrection at dawn.

And **The Poet** goes on...

* * *

Fruits of Hypomania / Brown Santa

2

Fruits of Hypomania / Brown Santa

Art facilitates

a temporary parole to my life

imprisoned in fear.

It produces so much love in my

heart.

I can't afford storage spaces,

so I keep giving it away.

* * *

This flesh and blood/I despise and despair.
My life is ending, it's beyond repair.

I want to be that copious vessel/that overflows without a sound.
Is it too late for me to understand art?
Should I live or end this circus?

The **Goddess of Muse** responded:

If a master you don't desire to be.
If a "student for life" in the mirror you don't see.
Don't call yourself an artist.

It's good that you found art attractive.
Wait for the day, it accepts your attraction.

From that moment on;
Every thought will be an inspiration, for creation.
Awake in your sleep/it will become your drug recreation.

Thread by thread/locked under your skin.
Thick questions you will shred and
Don't try to understand art.
Just let it take over your heart.
The whole of it...
not just a part.

* * *

The seed of muse/lies dry confused.

Force-fed worthless fiats.

The seed of muse,

is shredding the slag from youth.

Refining the ore/Grinding the core.

Overlooking science/lies inside my soul.

A Galaxy modern from time.

* * *

In my "Hermitty" life/There is something I can do/
Better than anyone else/
Minding my own business.

My life is a work of fiction.
But no character is intended to portray
any person or combination of persons/
living or dead.

My life is a work in progress.
My life is art.
Art, I don't pursue. I don't make.
It gets made, through me.

In my "Fictitious" life, I sleep enough.
But only in my dreams.
So, you may call me lucky... **One day.**

* * *

Rip the blinds/off your blessed eyes.
Embrace your unfashionable **Imperfections.**
Follow the mighty thread/guiding you through
the universal labyrinth.

* * *

Drown in envy and die with desperation
<u>Or</u>
Rise with inspiration and sink in creation.

cuz, mere desperation/

without any attempt at creation/

is a fool's action/

to recover a debt from life/

which was never due in the first place.

* * *

If you are broke, however, still proud to be a creator.
Welcome to this theater.

If you are wondering half of the day,
Rent is due, who can I borrow money from? Options are
few/what do I do? I have no clue
and why do I stare, everywhere?
Let me confirm. Yes! Your breed is one of the rare.

If you take everything around you/along with everything
that doesn't even surround you/very seriously but no one
seems to care. This is your story I am about to share.

Take a deep breath and look into the mirror/
Not just to find what needs to be fixed/
but unravel some thoughts intermixed.

You dream big, don't you?
Your steps are small, aren't they?
You dream big and your steps are small;
You need to jump but you hardly **Crawl**.

You are dying for advice/from people desperate to be wise.
But you are firmly aware/they can't guide you how to rise.
Because?

Faces differ BUT bullshit is same.

Life beats your game/you forget your name.

You are busy staring at walls and sky.

Your lowest wishes seem so high.

You sit in your car all alone,

Thinking like hell and scrolling your phone.

Let me rephrase that!

I sit in my car all alone/

To avoid thinking/I scroll my phone.

Then Music becomes nothing more than noise.

I scream in my head and I lose my voice.

Lonesomeness kills me/crowds, I avoid.

Thoughts in my head/run like a hamster on wheel on steroids.

My actions are empty, my thoughts are blind;

In this city of Angels, A friend is hard to find.

Dead dreams are crawling, under my skin.

Every Now and then, they Phoenix up to the pores.

When there is not enough space left for me, in my own core.

My heart is empty, nobody hears me shout;

Buried in me, no one can dig me out.

And then I start killing time; Ooooohhhhhh baby I kill time...

I take my time to kill time

I kill time knowing, it's killing me back.

cuz, maybe...trust in myself is all I lack.

You know, when I was a baby.

I didn't know how to walk.

I was looking at everyone walking around but I couldn't.

I tried but I couldn't so I did what I could

I crawl, I crawl and I crawl.

Every time I tried to walk, I would fall.

Everyone kept telling me I could walk/So I kept trying.

My knees hurt but I kept crawling.

Then something magical happened /They gave me a helping hand and said yes you can walk.

Yes baby yes, You can do it.

You can walk. You can walk.

And I finally walked and It was awesome!

Ooohhh I love walking.

They said watch your steps

I kept walking. Ooohhh I love walking/ Now I want to run.

They said watch your speed/"FUCK THAT".

I fell /I got up again, and I run and I run and I run.
Oohhh I love running, Now I want to fly.
They said ... NOOOOOO! Watch your dreams. Don't even dare to try. You will fall flat on your face and scream/but no one will pick you up.

I am going to fall flat 6 feet under anyway
And no one will be able to pick me up/YOU will too.

So, if you dream big and your steps are small?
Let them be small!
Before we all started walking
and running
and god forbid flying
we all had to do what?

Exactly.

* * *

When you grow/Before you show/what you know.

Just check to see if your soul is free.

Just check, if you are grounded in your roots.

Just check, if you are wearing your boots.

Storms will head your way,

Storms you have never seen,

Storms that will shake your being.

But they will prepare you for what you can't yet see.

In those **Storms.**

No one can help you.

No one will help you.

No one should help you.

It's your battle, you will have to fight.

Greatness is your right and rights are never given,

but taken.

* * *

Art is a pure expression of emotion.
Least of sleep and endless devotion.
In bits and pieces,
I do numerous senseless thesis.
They say you have to love it
until your heart, breaks.

I didn't hear any sound;
Neither any blood was found;
But I swear on god if he exists.

When I just let it happen;
not forcing a gist,
My fingers bleed,
when I don't resist.

* * *

Don't be the one

who grow

just to show.

Don't be the one

who doesn't show

what he knows, either.

For, **A spell untold**

is no good

to a cursed soul.

* * *

Fruits of Hypomania / Brown Santa

If all you can see around you;
is everyone else's destination, but your's.
Believe me, you are not blind.
You are going where you are supposed to go.
A Lion walks in pride
You ain't no sheep, to follow behind.

Forgive your past, don't forget your past.
Plan your actions, not the future itself.
After forgiving and planning,
Keep Coming back to "Now".
It's slipping from your hand
Grab it like "**Handful of sand**".

Keep sipping from minds deeper than Wells.
Bless every breath/Bless every bite.
Bless who did you wrong/Bless who did you right.
And Dust yourself off/When you fall in a fight

Who else shall pick you up,
if not you?

* * *

It's the arrival of the end of **lap three**.

Yet, I never knew/

that my mother always knew/

that I didn't knew/

How to fill the gap between/

What people think, say, and do.

Let me redo my wiring.

Let the battle begin from the beginning.

Let me count, my two ears and four eyes.

I never knew Vagitus was my countdown/

To sprint this marathon of precarious respiration/

in a loop of tunnel/without a vision.

* * *

3

The following poems are for a girl
who doesn't wear any make-up on her skin or her soul.

I told you I will write a poem for you.
I broke my promise
I wrote many

Fruits of Hypomania / Brown Santa

a little love made

a not so simple life

a little less complicated.

How do I know, I love you?

Because our goodbyes are longer than our hellos.

I implore you, to be the virtuous canvas.

No man, Woman or Deity ever possessed.

I am he who will paint on you/

My every color suppressed.

I should have saved for you, all the moves.

To rhyme with your rhythm, without a blink.

Take me by the anchor/In you, I wish to sink.

* * *

Let me call you an itch,

I am dying to scratch

but I don't want you to go away.

I am the broke artist-type/

your mother warned you about/

Suffering from a condition called unconditional love.

And what is suffering for love/but love itself?

I am looking for a heart,

for which I won't have to win this world,

but be its world.

I promise to love you more than I hate myself.

cuz, what's the point of love

if I can't die for it?

Or at least,

if it doesn't kill me.

* * *

We both love ice-cream.

There were lots of options to choose from.
A few of them reached my lips
but I left them right there.

Some were too sweet, Some too sour.
Some made my eyes roll,
Some took away from me all my power.
Some/easy to forget,
Some/deep regret.
Some tasted like wine, but cheap brand.
Some were like sonnets, hard to understand.
Some were like Sonata, under the moonlight.
Some were like headache, from a senseless fight.
But, my tongue keeps pulling me back to,
what it is addicted to.
A flavor, I left far behind.
You are sweet/most of the time,
with the right amount of sour.
You are just the right kind.
With you, I can afford to fall blind.

I said it then, I will say it again:

I never considered you another score.

No one, but you;

Left me hungry for more

Just like ice-cream.

Just like ice-cream

after it was over

My tongue is left cold and numb

Covered in what

is left of you.

* * *

I will be **Your boomerang**.

But,

I am afraid

I might lose track

On my way back

into your hands.

***

I am the scratched record,
that gets stuck more often than it wants
to.

I love the sound of you.
Had I been able to dance on any other
tune,
I wouldn't have fallen for you.

There's a rhythm that you have
which is hard to find.
But, the problem is
We both are in love,
with what I found.

***

I am not afraid when we differ in taste.

But,

When you serve me every dish I crave.

I am not afraid when things are unclear

But,

When you to tell me everything I want to hear.

I am not afraid when you display all your colors.

But,

When you paint the perfect portrait you think I wish to see.

I am not afraid when you tell me you love everything I do.

But,

When you don't hate anything about me.

I am sand/you made a castle out of me

But,

I can't let you crush me;

I can't let you complete me.

So, I volunteer to be the ocean as well.

I am afraid, we are perfect for each other;

We both love crushing perfection.

* * *

Follow your head.

not that **dummy**—

the one on your shoulders.

* * *

They say love is magical
AND
it was.
Those breaths we synced,
is the only life I remember living.
BUT
Your magic stinks.
I don't even need to look;
I can smell your tricks.
AND
I know People will hurt you.
Pretending they are hurt,
when they know, you get hurt,
from them getting hurt.
BUT
I would love to go back
to be an emotional fool.
Now I know why they don't teach us
the language of eyes in school.
AND
My brain keeps telling me, "it's not your loss."
BUT
what do I tell my heart,
who doesn't deal in maths?
AND
They say love is in the air.
They never say it's just as polluted.
BUT...

* * *

...I agree I must be losing my mind,
How can you do something
you have never done before.

You just don't know,

how not to deceive.

* * *

I did when I could,

I do when I can,

I won't because I can't, Anymore.

Let your **Bullshit** fly.

Because I would have been,

if I could have been.

But, I am not wired to be

another feather in your cap

* * *

It's my fault.

I did it.

I did it again.

But, I don't know

if I should be sad or proud.

Since I am an **Expert**

in disappointing.

***

I have ripped off/layers of skin/to rub off/
what you wrote on it/
years ago/With your fingers.

Leaving was easy,
Not going back took **Courage**.

* * *

To you

he is

what you were

to me.

To him

you are

what I am

to you.

To her

he is

what you are

to him.

God is Great.

* * *

I am already sinking in self-loathing, and

she updated her status:

"I want to be hated today."

To be honest, you didn't need to ask for it.

I am aware of your intentions,

but still, I will grant you your wish.

When was the last time I didn't?

Hating you is how I punish myself

for learning the same lesson;

over

and over

and over

And Over.

* * *

Don't seek attention.

Don't seek respect.

Don't seek love.

Pay Attention to the one

who loves to respect you.

In whose presence

you don't have to prove yourself.

In whose presence

you can afford to be incomplete

and

less than

what everyone else

thinks you should be.

* * *

Love is like a Rubik's cube.

Whenever I solved it,
it wasn't interesting anymore.

So I **Messed it up**...again.

* * *

You were like a moment of silence
In the storm of my life.
A lot has died in me since then
but the fire is still keeping up
with the wind, somehow.

I am not afraid of the end.
I was afraid of an end without you
But, if not with you
at least I ended up
with a few logs of Poems
Because of You
and they keep me warm.

* * *

(Note: There's a saying in India that if you keep a dog's tail in a pipe for 12 years, It will still be twisted when you take it out.)

Even if I unblock you and text you first;
please, don't text me back.
I need to learn
to stop watering the dead plants, over and over.
I need to learn
they are dead for a reason.
I need to learn
to stop forgetting the reasons.
I need to learn
to stop letting you break, what you don't own.
I need to learn
to stop waiting for everything to break.
I need to learn
to put my broken pieces back together, myself.
I need to learn
to stop fixing everyone, with my broken self.
I need to learn
that there will always be something to learn.
One thing I have learned so far is that Love is much more stubborn than a dog's twisted tail.
So, if I text you this poem, You know what not to do.
But in case you want to,
It's ok.

* * *

Fruits of Hypomania / Brown Santa

Fruits of Hypomania / Brown Santa

4

Fruits of Hypomania / Brown Santa

I hate tobacco;

I can never get addicted to it.

(coughing...)

I am cutting down;

(Cooughing...)

I smoke only when I drink.

(COOOOughing...)

I am down to, a pack a day—

that's progress, right?

(COOOOOOOOughing...)

How many times do I have to tell you?

I am not addicted!

I just need one...to poop.

(COOOOOOOOOOOOOOOOUGHING...)

Let me smoke, for god's sake;

we all gonna die anyway.

COUGH.

* * *

Character is like "Sun".

It will burn your core,
but it makes you shine.

Except,

it doesn't show up every morning

by itself.

* * *

(A conversation I had with a First Generation Indian American Tinder date)

After talking for a while about Blah Blah Blah...

She: Your English is very good.
I: umm.. I think it's alright.

She: How long have you been here?
I: Some days it feels like yesterday.
Some days it feels like eternity.
Depends on the kind of day I am having
But if you are asking numerically
It's been a few months over 4 years.

She: WOW... you don't sound like an **FOTB**
I: hmmm?
She: Which 7/11 do you work at?
I: what?
She: I mean where do you work?
I: I will tell you that but What's FOTB?
She: Oh, forget I said it
I: Why? What does it mean?

She: Umm.. I don't mean to offend you but FOTB means
Fresh off the boat.

I: Ohhh... I am not offended, I get it.
You mean I don't sound like your father!
(You should have seen her face, lol)
I am sorry, I don't mean to offend you
I am just kidding.
I am totally fine with sounding like an FOTB Or not.
But you definitely sound like an M.A.T.A.

She: Now what is MATA?
I: Ohh forget it.. I don't wanna offend you
She: No.. please tell me
I: Well... the kids of FOTB's Who sound
"More American than Americans"
are called MATA's.
(You should have seen her face again. She picked up
her fancy bag along with her fancy ass
and was about to storm out.)
I: Before you leave...I don't work at a 7/11
It's a Liquor Store.

***

I am unable to understand

Why **Some people hate life.**

It's just about

pre-school,

elementary school,

viral videos,

teenage crisis,

high school,

graduation,

job,

mid-life crisis,

marriage,

sleep-sucking monsters,

car loan,

home loan,

personal loan,

credit-card bills,

constipation pills,

asthma pump,

unwanted lump...

And at the cliff of life

preach everyone "how to live"

Spend all your life afraid to jump.

Stop complaining already!

***

We all are **Born Undocumented**

and

We die without notice.

Love,

Rage,

Joy,

Melancholy,

and every other ineffable,

inexplicable,

un-namable emotion is not patented to

any caste, color, religion, Or creeds.

All that differentiates us,

are good or bad deeds.

But,

Until our tongues

keep addressing you and me

as your people and my people

but us people

There will never be justice

for all people.

* * *

What you used to be

was a different person.

What you are right now

is a different person.

What you want to be

will be a different person.

So, if they don't recognize you anymore;

congratulate yourself.

For, how far you have reached

on the **Journey towards YOU**

from their perception of you.

* * *

Everyone was relatable,
When **I wasn't myself.**

They say I am ineffable;
Now, that I can't be anyone else.

But, If my words have weight,
They will sink in the right mind.

* * *

The biggest tragedy in my life is:

"I will do it **Tomorrow.**"

* * *

God: What do you want from me?

I: I want YOU...

I: What do you want from me?

God: **Let go** of I

* * *

The question is, do we need religion?

Let me put it this way.

Let's say Religion is a Pizzeria and spirituality is the Pizza.

Now, if you tell me that there is only one chain of Pizzeria's who make the world's best pizza.

Either YOU are Stupid or you think I am Stupid or you don't think at all or you have outsourced your thinking. Or you think like a dead man's clenched fist.

Make sense? No? Yes?

Let me put it this way.

Every religious man

is not necessarily spiritual

And

Every spiritual man

doesn't necessarily have to be religious.

You can learn to cook your own pizza.

So what do we need religion for?

Obviously for the ones who like home delivery and pizza is life.

There's no life without Pizza but if you don't like what your Pizzeria is cooking. Get out of it. cuz what you eat and where you eat from is no one's business but yours.

The freedom of Individuality is what makes us Humans.

Religions exist for humans.

Humans don't have to exist for religions.

Let me put it this way,

Let's say religion is a school

and

spirituality is your degree

But, if you never graduate,

school is your new prison.

Am I connecting the dots?
No? Yes?
Let me put it this way, for one last time

A **Religion**

If

doesn't lead you to the doorstep of the universe

but be the universe itself.

It's nothing more than a Propaganda...

P.S: I personally love Jalapeño, onion, and pineapple with Basil pesto sauce on a thick base. I like thick base

* * *

…There is no leaf on a tree

Which resembles the other

Yet they sing in harmony

When god whistles through them.

I wonder if they are **Religious.**

∗ ∗ ∗

Oblivion's desert is the **Mirage of life.**
Under my heels, are the grains of truth,
smirking at my fight.

Lacking aesthete are the boisterous neat.

Complacent corpses
keep crawling in dust,
until they rust,
to become grotesque dust.

* * *

Uncertainty and ambiguity about the execution of **Intentions** behind the words, we spill will never take anyone anywhere.

* * *

I don't know

if I have always seen the **Tragedy** coming

Or

It comes because I am always expecting

it.

* * *

Hide **Your Charities**,

like you hide your anomalies.

Let him choose your payback,

For, his blessings are greater than

your paeans.

* * *

5

This poem is for my mother.
We have shared lots of life-changing experiences that have shaped life for good or bad but this is one experience, I don't wish on anyone for good or bad.

Fruits of Hypomania / Brown Santa

I asked my mother,
"Mom, how much more than a man, is a woman's skin thick?"
"Were you born with four eyes, or is it some kind of trick?"

She held my face in her hand and replied,
"It's a wall of defense, son. Throughout my life,
I ended up building, brick by brick."

Let me share a story from seven seas away when I was 8. My mother picked me up at the school gate. We were power walking home on that empty street cuz my stomach is empty and I gotta eat. When right in front of us came a bunch of guys, in a jeep. Hunting for some skin, They were mistaking my mother for a sheep.
She locked her left hand around my wrist, Her right hand has become a fist and She screamed her way out of it/punching left and right.
Scream is a weapon my mother inherited from her mother.
A weapon she was taught to keep it sharp and loud, ready up her sleeve. I was too young to understand/That day, she just learned the meaning of **dodging a bullet** or maybe that's the first time I saw it happening. That day, When those neutered fuckers decided to have some fun. Mama, I wish you had a gun to finish the business undone. I am not a violent person. But, I wish to find each one of them. If age hasn't yet, put them to sleep. I will slit their throats on the same street. Maybe, then I will be able to delete; in my every vein this raging heat.

I am not a violent person.
But, let me teach you how to be useful in a much-forgotten fashion. What lies on top of your wrist, when divided is called a hand. But, when brought together; it becomes an independent union of fingers, it's called a fist. And it's meant to rise in the air/when your conscience takes a hit.

When the woman who made news wasn't your Eve.
It's not my problem, was your gut belief.
First of all, let me clarify: That wasn't your gut belief.
It was just an easy option available up your sleeve. Easy is a word that doesn't come easily to me. I learned my lesson the hard way.
So, When you see something/don't just post something/ Motherfuckers, do something.
If the sun on your side is still shining,
it doesn't mean it won't set. It just means it's not your turn, yet.
And at your dusk, Everyone should rescue you/This is what you are hoping, I bet.

But, if you are chilling when your neighbor is burning
it's only a matter of time you ignorant ass fuckers,
You will regret.

* * *

I am not a violent person.

But, don't mistake me for **Gandhi.**

I won't turn the other side of my face,
if you push me to the other side of grace.

* * *

Sometimes I weep but my tears have no one to

blame.

The ineffable/unspoken sit on my tongue

for ages.

It denies finding its way in ink,

a rightful space to claim.

Sometimes, the ocean,

the trees,

the fallen leaves,

the flowers in the breeze,

leaves me with **Poems, I can never write.**

* * *

Fruits of Hypomania / Brown Santa

About the Author

When I look into the mirror, I don't recognize myself. I don't know who is this guy in the mirror who is staring at me, but I will try my best to explain.

Born and raised in Bathinda, Punjab (India). I and my town used to be very small and slow. I am not small anymore and my town is not slow anymore.
My entire life I haven't achieved anything at all. I have been a failure at everything and anything. Chubby like a bean bag I was never an athlete, I hated school and every book that I had to cram to barely get passing marks. I am unable to pay attention to something that doesn't interest me. I wouldn't call it a disability but it's definitely an ability, that I never had.
I have the most terrible memory possible. I can't remember shit and I love it.
I suck at multitasking. I enjoy geographic dyslexia.
I have a very one-track mind but I had no idea which track I wanted to walk in life. So, while I was figuring out what I don't want to do. In the meantime, I graduated in 2014 from Law School (Panjab University, Chandigarh).
Growing up in a middle-class family in India, the priority of the parents was to make sure that their son will be able to put food on the table and any career in Arts was like a march towards starvation.
I was such a troublemaking and dull kid, I remember my father yelling at me, "You are going to be nothing more than a beggar". I don't blame him, he has risen from the bottom of the bottom and was venting fear, not hate. I love my father.

Writing has always been an outlet for my insanity. It helps me co-habitat in this perfect world. The liberty with writing is, I don't need anyone else to bring my ideas to life.
I love my mother who always believed in me. She is my rock and my heart. She is the most patient and loving human I have ever met in my life. (I never said it you mom but let me say it now, I LOVE YOU.)

Long story short, I packed my bags and moved to Los Angeles in 2015 to study Method Acting at The fabulous Strasberg Institute (WeHo). Acting stirred the creative juices which lead to falling back in love with long lost Poetry.

I don't know where this journey is taking me but I am very grateful where I am, spiritually. I haven't been home since 2015 and I miss Punjab. I don't know when I will be able to visit back but LA is second home now.

If you are reading this, I hope I will meet you someday and shake your hand or get a hug. I am a hugger. Take good care of yourself. There's only one of you.

Brown Santa

Fruits of Hypomania / Brown Santa

Podcast:

English: Brown Santa Rants

Punjabi: ਮੈਂ ਸਾਬੂ ਬੋਲਦਾਂ (Sarab Gill)

Email: iambrownsanta@gmail.com

(Please Use Pg 1 to write your review.)

Made in the USA
Monee, IL
26 August 2019